207 Inspirational Quotes of Charles I. Prosper

Charles I. Prosper

First Edition • April 2015

Global Publishing Company • Los Angeles, California

207 Inspirational Quotes of Charles I. Prosper

Charles I. Prosper

Copyright © 2015 by Charles I. Prosper
All Rights Reserved

NO PART OF THIS BOOK MAY BE REPRODUCED, IN WHOLE OR IN PART, IN ANY FORM BY ANY MEANS, DIGITAL, ELECTRONIC OR MECHANICAL, INCLUDING PHOTOCOPY SYSTEMS, WITHOUT PERMISSION IN WRITING FROM THE AUTHOR. ADDRESS INQUIRIES TO GLOBAL PUBLISHING COMPANY, 2658 GRIFFITH PARK BLVD, SUITE 349, LOS ANGELES, CA 90039, OR TO PROSPERME7@HOTMAIL.COM

Book layout design and cover design by Charles I. Prosper

LIBRARY OF CONGRESS CATALOG CARD DATA

ISBN–13 978-0-943845-22-7

PRINTED IN THE UNITED STATES OF AMERICA

12 11 10 9 8 7 6 5 4 3 2 1

Dedicated to Luzemily, my beautiful daughter and best friend

Contents

Introduction. vii

On Spirituality. 1

On Happiness.. 91

On Prosperity.. 117

On Problem-Solving.. 127

On Success 147

On Goals 189

On Health. 197

On Relationships 201

About The Author 225

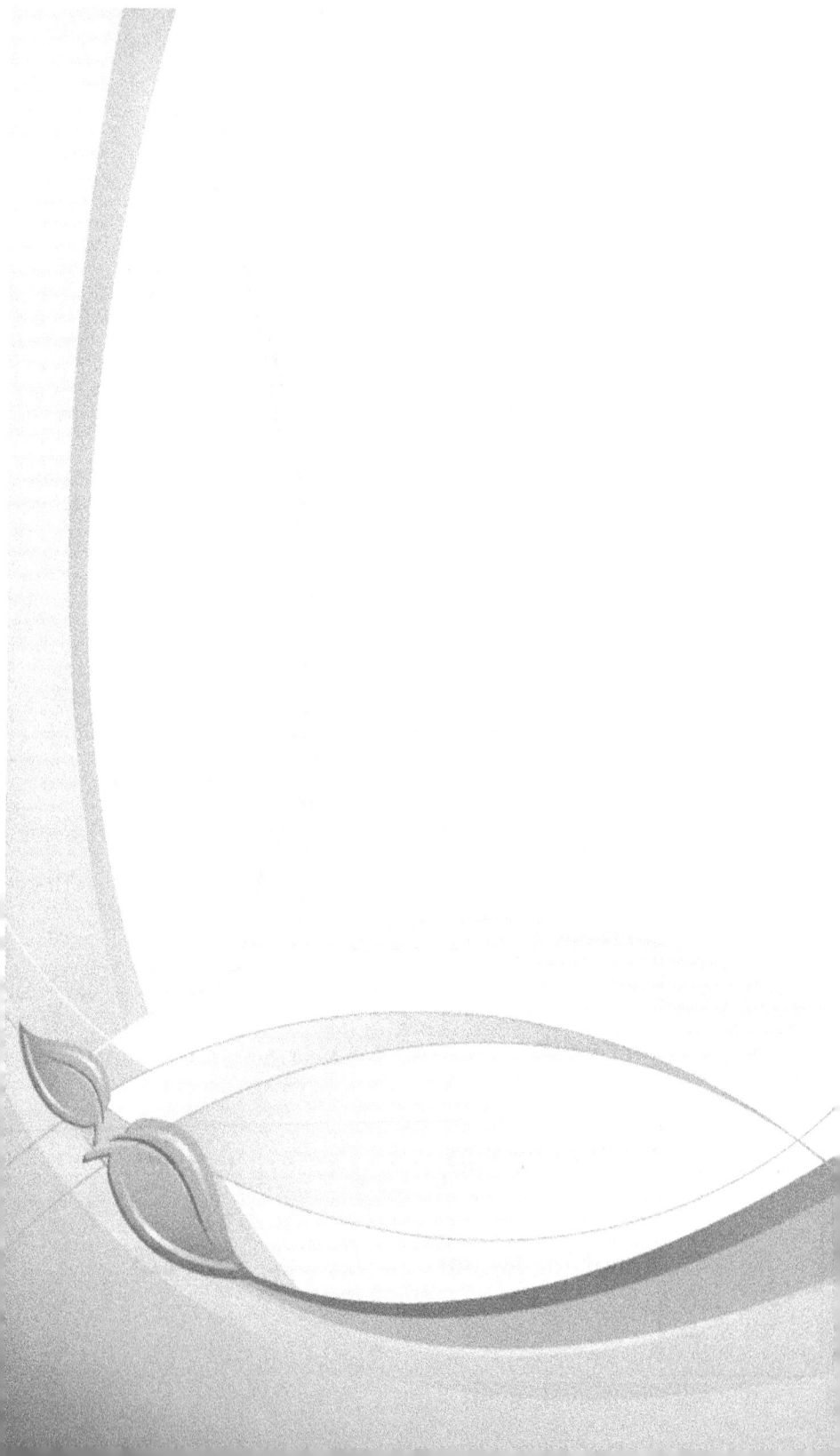

INTRODUCTION

I did not sit down and decide to create this book all at once in one sitting or in several sittings.

This book of 207 quotations was given to me in post-meditative moments or just spontaneously when I was not thinking about anything in particular over the course of 21 years.

By no means can I expect that you will believe or accept everything that I have written here in this book, but if it stimulates your thinking to go a little deeper within, then I have achieved my purpose in writing it.

I realize that you could read or "finish" this book in less than 10 minutes, however, it was written not to be quickly read or finished, but rather that the thoughts contained on each page be meditated upon and revisited again and again whenever needed.

You could easily spend one day or one week on any one thought and thus experience a life-transformation.

So start, anywhere in the book, and allow yourself to be drawn to what you need to know at that moment.

Blessings to you and to those whom you love most.

Charles I. Prosper
March 9, 2015

207 Inspirational Quotes of Charles I. Prosper

On Spirituality

Belief is a gold coin with faith on one side and patience on the other.

• ON SPIRITUALITY •

For God hears best those from whose lips come the words that are carried by the wings of gratefulness.

God answers prayer through opportunity.

• ON SPIRITUALITY •

Because God is everywhere, we can see him anywhere.

Many great opportunities come in the form of problems.

• ON SPIRITUALITY •

Worry is a mild form of temporary atheism.

You don't have to be religious in order to pray. You only have to be willing to listen within.

• ON SPIRITUALITY •

Do not look to God for something you're not willing to do for yourself.

Reality is that which exists independent of your perceptions of it.

• ON SPIRITUALITY •

Happiness comes from your mind. Peace comes from God.

Memory is no more than what you believed happened.

• ON SPIRITUALITY •

Exactly, how long does the present moment last?

Does time really exist, or is it God's momentary magic act?

• ON SPIRITUALITY •

The mayfly's short life-cycle is 12 hours – from morning to the evening. Is 12 hours to the mayfly the same illusion as 85+ years to us?

God is in control of coincidences as God is in control of randomness.

• ON SPIRITUALITY •

People want proof, and then they squabble on the definition of proof.

Sometimes God answers our prayers by not giving us what we ask for.

• ON SPIRITUALITY •

Even a "coincidence" happens for a reason.

"Going to church," for some relieves the responsibility of loving their fellow man with patience, kindness, and forgiveness.

• ON SPIRITUALITY •

Your life is the perfect metaphor of your beliefs.

You can decide to be happy, but you must pray for peace and guidance.

• ON SPIRITUALITY •

The experience of love, peace, or joy removes the need to experience time.

Gratitude is its own reward.

• ON SPIRITUALITY •

It's okay to say "I don't know" while trusting that the answer will come.

God is closer to you than you are to yourself.

• ON SPIRITUALITY •

If you trust God, you will find that God can be trusted.

God surrounds and speaks to us in the language of infinite opportunity.

• ON SPIRITUALITY •

Faith is trusting God and the flow of life without having to know where it is taking you.

Consciousness is God's currency.

• ON SPIRITUALITY •

There's a difference between knowledge and wisdom. Wisdom is knowing what's important and what's not.

*Trust
the flow
to always know —
which way
it is for
you —
to go.*

• ON SPIRITUALITY •

Knowledge is not power. Wisdom is power.

When religion contradicts common sense, they become mutually exclusive.

• ON SPIRITUALITY •

Wisdom comes when you ask, "Is this truly important?"

Answers to our prayers sometimes come in the form of knowing what questions to ask ourselves.

• ON SPIRITUALITY •

God will always help you even though your definition of "help" may be different than God's.

Consciousness is God.

• ON SPIRITUALITY •

What I need to know now is what I need to know now. What I need to know later will be different from what I need to know now.

Instinct is intelligence without intellect.

• ON SPIRITUALITY •

God is just you believing what to want to experience.

Nothing is something. Why do you pay for "empty" parking space?

• ON SPIRITUALITY •

I'm going to stop trying to know; I'm just going to go with the flow.

When you detach from immediate results, become patient, and trust in the ultimate good outcome of your life situations, it becomes a way of loving God.

• ON SPIRITUALITY •

I did all I could with what I understood – and that's all life expects of me. Now, I let go, and let God.

Act before you can think of reasons why you shouldn't, and courage will be yours.

• ON SPIRITUALITY •

What's important to know or to do is relative to what you need to know or to do at the moment.

Some people feel that because they read the Bible, it is exactly the same as living it.

• ON SPIRITUALITY •

Coincidence is the study of how God operates.

We hear God in silence as he speaks to us through the opened windows of our feelings.

It is in silence that we can hear God and the deeper the silence, the more we can hear.

There is nothing out there in this illusion that we call reality that can bring me peace but myself.

· ON SPIRITUALITY ·

Perception is reality relative to he who perceives it.

Coincidences are your personal metaphors of waking life.

• ON SPIRITUALITY •

Where would God be in a world where you had no problems?

Coincidence is the language of God.

• ON SPIRITUALITY •

My belief is God unto myself.

Choice is a continuous act until the event occurs.

• ON SPIRITUALITY •

Religion does not have to be logical to be believed.

Everything is coincidence, and God is in the middle managing it all.

• ON SPIRITUALITY •

When you believe in luck, you believe in God, since God is that which controls all luck.

Faith is not argued. It is only believed. That's what makes it powerful, mysterious, and miraculous.

• ON SPIRITUALITY •

Live in the present moment. That's where God is. That's where God lives.

Prayer doesn't "change" God. God is perfection and therefore changeless. Prayer changes you, and when you change, your world changes also.

· ON SPIRITUALITY ·

When you pray, however you pray — pray, and then become silent. You will be surprised at what happens next.

Whenever you want to be alone, whenever you want to be by yourself, you are feeling the presence of God.

• ON SPIRITUALITY •

Your religion is how you live your life.

All religions are philosophical attempts to explain how the universe works and how we interact in it — including the religion of science.

Atheism is another type of religious view which includes a non-participatory concept of God.

With faith, all things are possible.

• ON SPIRITUALITY •

Why problems? If you are never given the opportunity, how can your faith be developed?

Nothing is knowable beyond that which is not believed without doubt.

• ON SPIRITUALITY •

God is a mirror reflecting itself in another mirror.

Waiting is one of the many pursuits that our minds create in the pursuit of something more or "better" than the present moment.

• ON SPIRITUALITY •

Life's quiet beauty is often found in the face of a flower.

Thank you, God, for the joy of creation.

• ON SPIRITUALITY •

*This gift of life is on loan,
a moment we have but don't own —
A dream from which we will wake,
with all the memories we make.*

As I am growing older, my faith in God is deepening and my dependence on people, things, and circumstances is lessening.

• ON SPIRITUALITY •

Be patient with God. Hasn't he been patient with you?

The necessary things will create the necessary things for the necessary things.

• ON SPIRITUALITY •

If you knew exactly when something would happen for that which you believed, faith would not be necessary, and patience would be impossible.

Worry is the feeling when you tell God "I don't trust you."

• ON SPIRITUALITY •

When you do the right thing, the right thing always happens.

Bless you and thank you are synonymous.

• ON SPIRITUALITY •

Bless the problem to see your solution.

Student and teacher are two sides of the same coin.

• ON SPIRITUALITY •

I chose to use my power of choice.

Prayer is a state of peaceful awareness, regardless of the words that you say or not say.

• ON SPIRITUALITY •

"God" answers prayers through opportunities and ideas, but we change our lives through choice and right action.

On Happiness

Every moment you enjoy is a moment you will remember.

• ON HAPPINESS •

Keep it simple, and keep it consistent.

To be wise is to be happy. Wisdom is knowing what's important and what's not.

• ON HAPPINESS •

Freedom is being able to live without the demand of your desires.

Happiness does not ever result from inertia, or doing nothing, but rather from a conscious choice and an effort to move in a certain goal-fulfilling direction.

• ON HAPPINESS •

Boredom is when your only problem is that you don't have any problems.

My happiness is my decision to live happy moment-by-moment.

· ON HAPPINESS ·

You don't need what you want.

Never complain how heavy your groceries are.

• ON HAPPINESS •

Music is a mood of the human spirit embodied in the tonality of sound.

Most of us wish for things we already have.

• ON HAPPINESS •

I am blessed to the degree that I recognize that I am already blessed.

Nothing is meant to make you happy — not marriage — not money — not anything. Only you are meant to make you happy.

• ON HAPPINESS •

Your happiness is just on the other side of your fears. Can you cross over?

*Don't waste you worry for tomorrow.
You'll only waste it in sorrow.
Your life is now — can't you see —
tomorrow is without a guarantee.*

• ON HAPPINESS •

Happiness
Has little to do –
with who –
but you.

That you should do something – anything – is just somebody's opinion.

• ON HAPPINESS •

One's experience of "enough" is relative to one's capacity for gratitude.

The power of the bill collector rests on the ability to stimulate a "fear" of losing the approval of a total stranger.

• ON HAPPINESS •

I can never predict what I should have done.

Preferences are temporal and illusory forms with which we play.

• ON HAPPINESS •

Happiness is highly overrated – more important is peace, which transcends both happiness and sadness.

You know something is right because it gives you a feeling of peace.

• ON HAPPINESS •

Wisdom is the highest form of intelligence because it transcends the need for knowledge.

On Prosperity

Wealth is the depth of your enjoyment of life.

• ON PROSPERITY •

How I will use the present moment is more important than what will happen in the future.

The concept of luck is as deep and as mysterious as the concept of God.

• ON PROSPERITY •

Your focus is your future.

A day is a Divine Dollar for which you can spend any way you wish.

• ON PROSPERITY •

Opportunities are created in the moment that you recognize them as such.

It is not how much you have but how much you enjoy of what you have is the true measure of your prosperity.

• ON PROSPERITY •

Luxury is less clutter.

On Problem-Solving

A problem can become an opportunity to serve others and to prosper.

• ON PROBLEM-SOLVING •

You can't fight the future. You can only prepare for it.

What's the difference between a problem, a challenge, and an opportunity? — Your choice of label.

• ON PROBLEM-SOLVING •

"Calm acceptance of what is" – is the first step to solving any problem.

Problem-solving is not for cowards.

• ON PROBLEM-SOLVING •

How many times in your life have you asked "Will I ever get out of this?" And how many times have you gotten out of it — only to ask the same question again?

Seeing what must be done requires no further thinking, only courage and faith to act at once.

• ON PROBLEM-SOLVING •

"Trying" is an excuse for not doing, being, and having.

If you have an excessive habit of "thinking about" doing something, you will create the illusion of having begun it.

• ON PROBLEM-SOLVING •

Too much analyzing is not good for you. What are the first four letters of analyze?

Problems create a relationship between you and God.

• ON PROBLEM-SOLVING •

Problems give your life meaning. It means that you need to be more creative, resourceful, and trusting of God and of yourself.

Whimps do not solve problems, only the courageous do.

• ON PROBLEM-SOLVING •

Is a problem good or bad? What makes a jigsaw puzzle fun?

Scientific discovery requires the willingness to try yet another experiment with what has been learned and carefully recorded.

• ON PROBLEM-SOLVING •

When you don't know what to do – do only what you can do, and see what happens. Do more of what works and less of what doesn't until your problem is inevitably resolved.

Massive positive action is the second step to solving any problem.

• ON PROBLEM-SOLVING •

God moves when you do.

On Success

It is more important to have the intention than knowing the steps of how to get you there.

• ON SUCCESS •

A willingness to see opportunities is the only requirement for them to exist.

Time is opportunity.

• ON SUCCESS •

Opportunities not quickly and courageously acted upon become your rationalizations, remorse, and regret thereafter.

Stay with the intention and the joy of doing, and you will get there; in fact, once you are following the joy of doing, you have already arrived.

• ON SUCCESS •

A powerful intention is more important than someone's plan of how to do it.

Luck is a factor of what I do or I fail to do in a timely and consistent manner.

• ON SUCCESS •

It's not important that you do everything, only the important things.

Don't set out to build a wall. Set out to place the perfect brick. In time, the wall will take care of itself.

• ON SUCCESS •

Whether something will be difficult or easy depends entirely on the belief of the person.

You get what you believe you deserve.

• ON SUCCESS •

From your determination springs forth the plan.

It's not what you know, but what you consistently do with what you know that makes a difference.

• ON SUCCESS •

The question is never, why doesn't this work; the question is how can I get this to work?

I am at the stage of my life where I know that the majority of people will never do what the minority of successful people are always willing to do.

• ON SUCCESS •

Most people are supposed to be "average;" otherwise how could above average even exist?

Trust your intuition before trusting the "experts."

• ON SUCCESS •

I do what I have to do and not what I feel like doing is my formula for success.

Sometimes the more you know, the less you do, and "knowing" becomes a substitute for doing.

• ON SUCCESS •

Perfectionists don't get things done because they are lost in the illusion of their perfection.

There is nothing more important than what I choose to do right now.

• ON SUCCESS •

Try something new, and let life teach you how to do it better.

The power of flow is not what you do; it is that you do. Once you decide to do something – do it. See what happens – then continue from there.

• ON SUCCESS •

Flow and success are synonymous.

To start something important, you don't have to wait until you have all of the answers. You only need the intention to learn, and learn you will.

• ON SUCCESS •

You need to believe positive while you are doing positive things. You can't believe positive while you are doing negative things.

Inspiration without immediate action is only a form of cheap entertainment.

• ON SUCCESS •

Improvement is better than accomplishment because accomplishment is only achieved through improvement.

Faith is the strength to stand up and face the problem. Courage is the will to continue. Success is the result.

• ON SUCCESS •

God wants you to succeed to the degree that you are willing to do whatever it takes to succeed.

It's what you do now that will determine your future, not what you think you can or will do at some time in the impossible "future."

• ON SUCCESS •

Your greatest challenge always comes just before your greatest victory. That's why you should never give up.

The three C's of success are: consciousness, commitment, and consistency.

• ON SUCCESS •

A willingness to see opportunities is the only requirement for them to exist.

You fail by succeeding at the wrong tasks. What is your life's purpose? Why are you here? What must you give before you leave this Earth?

• ON SUCCESS •

Consistency + patience = persistence. Persistence = success.

If whatever you do, things begin to get better, easier, and more doors open, you are on the right track.

• ON SUCCESS •

If whatever you do, things begin to get worse, harder, and more doors begin to close, you are on the wrong track.

Believe in a world of opportunities, and you will begin to see them where you had never seen them before – even though they have always been there staring you in the face.

• ON SUCCESS •

Doing a little creates an experience of knowing what works, rather than doing nothing and wondering what will work.

On Goals

The courage to be uncomfortable is the dynamic behind taking that first step toward the accomplishment of any important goal.

· ON GOALS ·

Whenever you must make a choice between two things, one will make you think a lot, and the other will make you feel peaceful. Choose peaceful.

Achieving goals is not about getting there; it's about going there.

• ON GOALS •

Choice is a continuous act until the event occurs.

I can't prove it until I do it.

• ON GOALS •

Did you know that 4 out of 5 porcupines make acupuncture their first career choice?

On Health

The body is characterized by inertia; it is either energized or degenerated by the mind.

· ON HEALTH ·

Youth is a mind game.

On Relationships

The quality of our lives is defined by the quality of our relationships.

• ON RELATIONSHIPS •

If you ever want to see how much people really love each other, just stand and watch at the arrival or departure gate of any airport in the world.

Your life is defined by those with whom you choose to make the memories of your life.

• ON RELATIONSHIPS •

No one can pressure you; only you can give in.

Life is way too short to be politically correct. Love who you must love. Believe what you must believe, and do what you must do.

• ON RELATIONSHIPS •

You don't realize the value of something until you lose it.

If daddies would hug their daughters more, they would need less boyfriends.

• ON RELATIONSHIPS •

In the final days of your life, it is not how much you have accumulated, but how many people you have comforted, cared for, and listened to that will matter.

Never date a bank teller — she always knows how much money you have.

• ON RELATIONSHIPS •

Woman was placed on this Earth for man to earn his right to go to heaven.

Good sex is not the 110th position. Good sex is good friendship without your clothes on.

• ON RELATIONSHIPS •

"Leaving lipstick on a man's cheek" is an unconscious territorial marking, triggered by ions of female evolutionary psychology.

You will never rise any higher than the friends you hang around.

• ON RELATIONSHIPS •

Gossip is a mean-spirited and cowardly form of judgment of people who are not present to defend themselves.

Kids take play very seriously.

• ON RELATIONSHIPS •

Why do we love to watch our children when they sleep?

A person cannot hide character any more than he can hide his coffee by pouring it into his pocket.

• ON RELATIONSHIPS •

The only purpose of "kidding" is to hide the truth.

The purpose of your relationship with another person is not to make you happy, but conscious of your ability to give.

• ON RELATIONSHIPS •

Your life is only as good as the people you serve.

Rather than expect, accept.

• ON RELATIONSHIPS •

A pregnancy may be "accidental," but all childbirth is on purpose.

About The Author

Charles I. Prosper trained in marriage and family therapy for two years at Northcentral University's graduate school in Prescott Arizona and holds a Masters Degree in Psychology.

He is an experienced life coach and relationship expert in the areas of personal development, success, marriage & family relationships, and the development of greater self-esteem.

He is also the author of *The 12 Laws of Success* (2015.)

If you would like to contact if you would like to attend one of Mr. Prosper's "Success Focus Groups" in the Los Angeles area, or if you are interested in sponsoring a Success Focus Group in your area, send an email to:

Charles I. Prosper
Los Angeles, CA 90039
Prosperme7@hotmail.com

for more information.

You may also call (323) 351-4516 and leave a voice message.

Thank you and all the best to you and those whom you love most.

www.ingramcontent.com/pod-product-compliance
Lightning Source LLC
Chambersburg PA
CBHW051821090426
42736CB00011B/1584